When Your C.... is ready to hear...

The Truth
~ About ~
Santa Claus

Written by Alan Barrington
Illustrated by Joe McCormick

The house creaked again. Daniel's eyes *popped* open. He jumped out of bed and ran to the window. He looked up into the sky, and down on his front yard. He looked on the roofs of his friends' houses. He searched *all* around, but he could *not* find what he was looking for.

Every Christmas Eve, children all over the world listen and watch for Santa Claus. It's the most *exciting* night of the year. But no matter how hard they listen, or how long they watch, children like Daniel *never* see Santa bring their presents on Christmas Eve.

(Do you ever listen for Santa Claus on Christmas Eve?)

Presents have been important ever since the very first Christmas. The Bible tells us that Wise Men saw the star of Jesus' birth, and came with gifts for the

newborn King. Giving presents to our friends and family is one of the ways that we celebrate the birth of our Savior on Christmas Day.

Most children, like Daniel, have parents to buy nice presents for them. Other children have grandparents or family to take care of them, and give them presents.

But some children don't have any parents or family. And some parents are not able to buy presents for their children.

A long, long time ago, a man named Nicholas saw how sad these children were. He knew that presents were not the reason people celebrated Christmas, but he also knew that presents make Christmas a lot of fun.

(Do you like to get presents on Christmas?)

Nicholas was a very kind and generous man. When he thought of all the children who would not receive any gifts, his heart was broken. Nicholas wished that he could do *something* to make these children happy on Christmas Day.

Suddenly, Nicholas had an idea! He decided that *he* would bring presents to the children.

(Do you think that this idea made Nicholas feel happy?)

Nicholas kept his plan a secret. When Christmas Eve came, he left presents for *many* children.

Nicholas did not want anyone to know where the presents came from. So, he wrote "from Santa Claus" on each gift and left them at night, near the decorations, where the children could find them.

Nicholas was *very* happy when he heard how surprised each child was on Christmas morning. His heart was filled with joy when he saw the children playing with their gifts.

He was so happy that he started making plans to give away *more* presents the next Christmas.

Every year, Nicholas gave away more and more presents to more and more children. Before long, everyone had heard of Santa Claus and his love for little ones.

Years later, people even made up songs about his white beard, and a sleigh full of gifts pulled by reindeer.

Santa Claus was so well known that he became a special part of our Christmas celebration.

After many years, Nicholas finally grew too old to give away presents.

But his message of helping people, and spreading the love of Jesus, with gifts, at Christmas-time was much too important to forget.

People everywhere knew that they had to help.

(What would you do to help?)

Parents all over the world wrapped presents and gave them to their children in the name of Santa Claus.

Some people delivered presents to orphans and the poor in the name of Santa Claus.

Because of this, the name of Santa Claus lived on even after Nicholas was not able to bring any more gifts.

He had taught all of us to love one another as Jesus did.

Every year, Daniel and his family celebrate Christmas together.

On Christmas Eve, they drink hot apple cider and sing carols around the Christmas tree.

Sometimes, Daniel's relatives come to visit, and his Dad reads the Christmas story to everyone from the Bible.

They *always* have lots of fun together.

(What does your family do on Christmas Eve?)

Christmas is *very* exciting for Daniel's parents, too.

All year long, they plan what they will do on Christmas Eve. They also plan the gifts they will give to their friends and family, and *especially* Daniel.

Nothing in the world could make them any happier than watching Daniel enjoy his new toys on Christmas morning.

After Daniel goes to bed on Christmas Eve, his parents wait until they think he is asleep. They look in on their son, to make sure that he is not still listening and watching for Santa Claus.

When they are certain that he is asleep, they take the presents out of their secret hiding place, and put them around the Christmas tree.

When Christmas morning comes, Daniel jumps out of bed and runs to the tree to see all the presents.

Then he wakes up his parents and everyone else in the house. Everyone is so happy as they share the fun, the love of Jesus, and all of the presents on Christmas morning.

We've learned a
lot about who Santa Claus
was, but we must never forget
the most important thing about
Christmas.

Even though Santa Claus does not
really bring our presents, Jesus is the
real reason we celebrate Christmas.

Jesus *IS* the Son of God, and He came to
earth as a little baby in a manger.

Jesus grew up and lived a perfect life as an example for us. Then He died on the cross to save us, so that we could live with Him in Heaven. But, He *never* said one mean word to the people who hurt him. He showed us that *everyone* deserves to be loved. And, everyone needs to receive the best gift of all—Jesus!